AF265331

Bitcoin & Black Powernomics

Will Hobdy

Bitcoin & Black Powernomics

Copyright © 2020 by Phalconstar

All rights reserved. No part of this book may be reproduced or transmitted in any form or by any means without written permission from the author.

ISBN: 978-0-578-23927-9
ISBN: 979869264372
ASIN: B08KH8CJ9J

Printed in USA

Dedication

This book is dedicated to America's Black newspaper publishers. Particularly, those in the state of Texas. Also, to their editors, writers, columnists, advertising sales professionals, designers, office support staffs and distribution team.

Thank you for continuously inspiring the art of putting ink to paper, decerning the times, recording our history and troubling the waters in quest for freedom and liberty.

Table of Contents

Preface

I first heard about Bitcoin (BTC)[1] in 2010 when a news story hit about a guy buying two pizzas for 10,000 Bitcoin. I was reminded of that event in late 2016 when a friend in California called and said that he and several business partners were researching Bitcoin mining and they were actually earning Bitcoin. At the time, Bitcoin was valued at about $600 per Bitcoin.

I started reading everything on Bitcoin that I could find and watching YouTube videos. There were not very many- at the time. I called him in early 2017, told him what I had learned and

---

[1] https://bitcoin.org/bitcoin.pdf

listened as he told me more about how the Bitcoin

mining math worked under the hood.

I was sold. The more I've learned about

Bitcoin, the better I understand that everything

about it is built around game theory, encrypted and

immutable math. It was like fire shut up in my

bones, it has been that way ever since.

Introduction

Bitcoin is a rare digital asset that is used to instantly transfer value over the Internet without interference from others, time or space. Bitcoin has the capability to be a formidable opponent to an outdated monetary system that was constructed for manipulation by systemic, institutionalized and discriminatory monetary policies. Bitcoin is based on game theory that favors fair-play and rejects corrupt behavior.

It is important that Black Americans begin exploring Bitcoin and blockchain technologies and keep abreast of world developments in this new asset class.

If the current monetary system continues to fail due to problems such as insurmountable debt, a pandemic, corrupt politics and more, Bitcoin represents our best hedge for producing value.

The political decision to remove gold as the value benchmark for the US dollar (USD) in 1971 signaled a new era of assault on African Americans and suppression for developing countries in Africa and South America. The time was reminiscent of America's great political Compromises of 1787[2] and 1877[3] that brought repeated misery to Black America.

---

[2] Three-fifths Compromise of 1787. Britannica.org
[3] The Compromise of 1877 Khanacadeemy.org

This political edict essentially created the crumbling monetary system we use today. Without the gold benchmark, a rising Black middle class in America and gold-rich under developed countries in Africa were segregated from a sound money and integrated into a US dollar (USD) dominated fiat monetary system that is now showing signs of impending failure. This is not a comprehensive or exhaustive economic treatise on Black Powernomics[4] but a catalyst for encouraging Black participation in Bitcoin technology and involvement in its development as an alternative platform for our value transactions.

---

[4] *Powernomics: The National Plan to Empower Black America* (2001) by Dr. Claud Anderson

Neither is this financial advice. But it highlights the damage created by an overly weaponized US dollar (USD) that has created increasingly stronger enemies abroad and greed at home that have contributed to undermining the US dollar's (USD) status as a global reserve currency.

Until recently, US policy makers had an unlimited ability to use the dollar as an instrument of controlling world politics. But since the 2008 financial crises and the rise of China as a world power, the US dollar's (USD) influence has rapidly deteriorated.

Bitcoin was an inspired response to that failure. At first glance, Bitcoin is a digital tool with many layers. It has a decentralized base that is universally proven to be tamper-proof. And, it has

demonstrated over the last 11 years that it is also a

provably-fair measuring tool for determining

value.

This book takes you beneath the hype about

Bitcoin and hopefully inspires people to empower

themselves, friends, family and community.

Remember, Bitcoin's universality lends to its

usefulness on a local as well as interconnected

global scale.

Bitcoin is also a digital unit of account that

creates its own network effect. A single Bitcoin

can be split into 100 million smaller fractions,

called satoshis.[5] There will only ever be 21 million Bitcoin (BTC). This means Bitcoin is scarce. Its integrity can also be proven by mathematical means as we will see later.

The Bitcoin ecosystem is comprised of computer programmers, developers, miners, node operators, merchants, owners, traders, exchanges, government regulators, financial technology companies, research firms and Bitcoin hoarders.[6]

Bitcoin's global community has room for poets, musicians, philosophers, artist and graphic designers and any who desires to employ their talents and creativity in contributing to Bitcoin's

---

[5] https://www.btcsatoshi.com/
[6] *Trusted Bitcoin Ecosystem* White Paper. June 2017

success because no single person or entity is in charge of its network, or its public relations.

But each day brings new developments to the Bitcoin world – a world where electronic devices are interconnected on a trust-less network that - until now - was science fiction. Such a network is said to have the potential to be the world's next dominate tool in determining value, just like computer technology has become the dominate tool in commerce and communications.

Over the last 11 years, the technological infrastructure required to make Bitcoin easier to use and digitally seamless has grown exponentially. These improved user experience developments are chipping away at the need for intermediaries, politicians and bankers to be in control of our affairs because Bitcoin has the capability of performing their function through consensus mechanisms.

These characteristics make it a trusted digital tool for securely digitizing and tabulating value transactions. Bitcoin decentralized ledger records near-real time confirmed transactions that are tamper-proof and beyond the control of any one individual or entity.

Since its creation in 2008, Bitcoin has operated atop the Internet, producing a steady supply of BTC cryptographic digits every 10 minutes, 24 hours a day, seven days a-week since 2009. This book does not go into the complex technical computer science of Bitcoin. It does, however, offer a glimpse into its cryptographic make-up and the provably-fair game theory that undergirds it.

Any references to businesses involved in digital currencies is for illustrative purposes to assist in understanding various business models and aspects of Bitcoin and other cryptocurrencies. Such references are not endorsements or recommendations.

Finally, a Bitcoin standard[7] deserves inquiry because what we value and engage in as humans have economic consequences.

---

[7] *The Bitcoin Standard: The Decentralized Alternative to Central Banking* by Saifedean Ammous

History of Bitcoin & Money

The idea of Bitcoin (BTC) emerged on an Internet message board in November of 2008 when a person or persons using the name Satoshi Nakamoto published a nine-page paper entitled, *Bitcoin: Peer-to-Peer Electronic Cash System*[8]. On January 3, 2009, Satoshi launched the free open-source Internet software for the Bitcoin protocol.

---

[8] https://bitcoin.org/bitcoin.pdf

As an open-source software, Bitcoin cannot be patented or trademarked but a variety of patented, trademarked and centralized private-label coins have been launched as fakes, alternatives and competitors to Bitcoin. So, understanding the basics of Bitcoin will help you understand the differences between Bitcoin and other so-called cryptocurrencies.

There was no fanfare or publicity when Satoshi's first Bitcoin genesis block was hard-coded onto the World-Wide Web. But for the first time in history, the world had what has become the most successful global decentralized cryptographic token and accounting system.

Today, technologies are under development that do not require Bitcoin's use over the Internet.[9] This space-based technology promises to provide areas around the world without reliable Internet connections the opportunity to use Bitcoin with a hand-held device.

For the past 11 years, the Bitcoin blockchain network has been successfully recording and validating Bitcoin inputs and outputs. The network is growing more secure and resilient each day according to Bitcoin metrics. And, since all Bitcoin transactions are available in near real-time, the achievement has been akin to safely,

---

[9] Blocksteam.com

continuously and routinely flying back and forth between the earth and moon without interruption.

Less than a year after sharing and testing the Bitcoin software with other computer scientists Satoshi vanished. It is well documented that Satoshi communicated with computer scientists such as Gavin Andressen, Hal Finney and others through message boards before going silent.

To this day, all the Bitcoins ever rewarded to Satoshi, including the first 50 BTC in the hallowed Bitcoin Genesis Block have never been moved or transferred. This decade of inactivity, coupled with accumulated unspent output in Satoshi's Bitcoin wallet make it doubtful whether he, she or them will ever return to take credit for inventing Bitcoin.

Bitcoin's history reveals that it is not only a powerfully secure, computerized digital platform but that it can also determine economic consequences and outcomes because money can be programed on top of its network. This technical architecture makes Bitcoin a sound money. And, sound money is important for global trade and cooperation.

For example, money was among the first technological tools devised by humans. It was a means of conducting trade across great distances. It offered the means and power to communicate and transfer value among regional groups. We know that money predates writing because some of the earliest samples of writing we have is of tallies, ledgers and pictures of debts owed.

It seems that writing was created just to explain who owned what. And, one of the first forms of expressing who owns what was barter exchange. In barter, we exchanged things like chickens for milk, or wheat for oil or whatever we owned with something someone else owned and wanted. Then, rare money tools like clay tablets, seashells, beads, stones and salt were used to communicate value.

Over a thousand years ago, precious metals like cooper, silver, and gold were based on monetary value. Coins minted with copper, silver and gold are such examples.

In the last 500 years, of Eastern and Western colonial and world empire powers, paper money, usually backed by precious metals emerged.

Over the last 100 years, centrally controlled banks, national governments and corporate controlled paper and plastic monies like bonds, credit, debit and payment cards emerged.

In the years following World-War II, the US dollar (USD) emerged as the world's reserve currency. In 1971, as the United States stood atop the zenith of world wealth when President Richard Nixon removed it from the $35 an ounce-gold standard. Other nations soon followed and by 1999, Switzerland was the last country to capitulate.

From that moment onward the idea of a US dollar (USD) being backed by American politicians, bankers and the military might of the United States government emerged. Experts say that once the Swiss capitulated, the world's fiat monetary system was destined to fail.

The most serious failure was the 2008 Financial Crisis. Today, world governments and central bankers are grappling with $250 trillion in global debt[10].   This is not sustainable.

---

[10] International Institute of Finance 2019 Report

Since the dawn of the computer different forms of digital money have been tried and thousands have failed. A few companies like PayPal have been successful in processing digital currencies but even so, it still requires banks or other trusted third parties for transaction permissions.

Amongst the chaos of the last four years, advanced digital computer technologies have been working to redefine the future of money. But the permission-less [no permission required] and decentralized architecture of the Bitcoin protocol offers a new paradigm shift that forces honesty and transparency in value transfers and rewards those who play fair. We will see later that it also punishes bad actors through consensus algorithms that detect and reject corrupt behavior and actions.

This new paradigm shift opens up a new world of possibilities for Black Americans and the world at-large because for first time in history, any person or company can instantly transfer value to anyone else anywhere on the planet without the aid and assistance of any bank, person or intermediaries. This had never been feasibly possible until Satoshi proved it with Bitcoin.

As mentioned earlier, the Bitcoin protocol quietly emerged from an Internet message board. By 2010, the first notable Bitcoin exchange transaction took place when Laszio Hanyecz of

New York sent 10,000 BTC to a citizen in Europe in exchange for two pizzas[11].

While the event did not capture the public's imagination for long, it did help to attract the likes of computer scientists, computer geeks, computer hackers, game theorists, cyberpunks, anarchists, cryptographers, libertarians and innovative thinkers who picked up on the open-to-the-public "decentralized" and "encrypted nature" of Bitcoin technology.

Over the next few years, economists in academia, entrepreneurs, financial technologists and investors around the world educated

---

[11]https://www.coindesk.com/bitcoin-pizza-10-years-laszlo-hanyecz

themselves and became involved with Bitcoin and helped build businesses and financial infrastructure around it.

And, by 2013, it was a billion-dollar market and attracting the attention of thousands of people, especially in Japan, China, South Africa and Zimbabwe. By 2017, it was a world-phenomena as it surpassed $200 billion in market value among some 50 million worldwide Internet users.

Nevertheless, Bitcoin is still new on the world stage and there is no guarantee that it will succeed, but it offers hope. Also, thousands of alternative cryptocurrencies now compete against Bitcoin for superiority and some of the biggest multinational corporations and institutions in the world are developing and building new infrastructure and industries inspired by it.

But Bitcoin stands alone in originality, organic network growth and decentralization. Bitcoin maximalist argue that alternative cryptocurrencies already have suffered or will eventually suffer the consequences of attempting to take advantage of Bitcoin's open-source code by creating and controlling their own centralized cryptocurrency. Still, billions of US dollars and other foreign currencies are pouring into investments to develop and build advanced financial infrastructure around Bitcoin and other cryptocurrencies.

Yet, Bitcoin remains unique in that it is not owned and controlled by any one person, entity, group, institution, corporation or government agency. Bitcoin owners are in control and are responsible for the safekeeping of their own Bitcoin.

P2P Electronic Cash System

As a peer-to-peer (P2P) electronic cash system, operating on the Internet, Bitcoin serves as both the cash and the bank. A Bitcoin enters the digital world through a process called mining. Once a Bitcoin has been mined it can be saved, spent, transferred, traded or sold.

Since a Bitcoin serves as its own cash and bank, every transaction is self-recorded on an open distributed public ledger called the Bitcoin Blockchain. All its transactions can be accomplished instantly and without the aid or assistance of a bank or any other intermediaries once onboarded on the Bitcoin platform. For better or worse, all confirmed Bitcoin ledger transactions are irreversible. So, handle with care.

Bitcoin owners receive crypto keys or crypto QR codes when they acquire Bitcoin-inputs. Users must also use crypto keys or crypto QR codes when they output - or sell, trade, spend, transfer or convert Bitcoin to cash.

I don't want to get too deep into the technical software aspects of Bitcoin, but here's basically how it works. Sending and receiving Bitcoin is similar in some ways to sending and receiving emails but Bitcoin can't be copied or duplicated. Instead of sending and receiving communicative messages with emails, the senders and receivers of Bitcoin send and receive units of value.

Technically speaking, in the 1990s if you wanted to send someone an email you had to hook-up your computer to a modem. Then you had to hook up your modem to your phone. Then you had to wait for everything to connect, then you could type and send your email, and a day or two later the receiver would receive it.

Well, we had to go through this long, drawn-out process because the technology was new - and better and faster Internet and email infrastructure had not yet been developed.

But in 1996, AOL introduced a $19.95 monthly Internet and email package and the modern email was born. Attaching documents, photos and videos to email would not develop and emerge until years later.

Today, most Bitcoin users can use various types of Bitcoin or crypto wallets to send, receive, and convert Bitcoin to fiat money simply by using their smartphone but the process of doing so can sometimes be awkward for people new to the technology just like it was for early emails.

Bitcoin's current development stands at about the same stage of development as early emails were before AOL popularized sending and receiving them. It is important to remember that early email technology was cumbersome for early users, too.

Still, Bitcoin is a valuable digital asset and rare commodity that people own and control. And, getting adapted to the responsibilities of storing and securing one's Bitcoin can prove to be a challenge for most people. Taking responsibility for your own Bitcoin can be a daunting task because we are used to relying on banks or other financial institutions for keeping our money and relying on them to deliver it to us when we request it.

On a good note, there are many new mobile phone Apps that are reliable for buying and storing small amounts of Bitcoin and other cryptocurrencies. The CashApp by Square is an example and other interface Apps with improved user experiences are growing in number.

Also, enterprising entrepreneurs are developing new businesses called Bitcoin custodial services to store large amounts of Bitcoin for individuals and institutions who may be unfamiliar or uncomfortable with handling a nonphysical digital asset.

Bitcoin's decentralized cryptographic make-up is another characteristic that makes it special as a peer-to-peer electronic cash system. When we want to apply value to our transactions, we usually turn to paper notes or fiat money for enumerations. As we move deeper into the digital age this millennia, we will increasingly turn to cryptographic enumerating tools for the security they offer.

Satoshi's gift to the world was this peer-to-peer electronic cash system for enumerations. It's a system on which the world's fiat currencies can be programmed to work on top of its high security network.

Most of the money supplied by central banks enters into the monetary system as nothing more than computer data created by banking authorities and computer keyboards as we will see.

Although it does not create digital fiat money, PayPal is one of the few fiat digital mcney payment systems that has enjoyed success in the

Western World while its chief competitor, Alipay enjoys success in China and the Eastern World. Apple Pay and Google Pay also are experimenting with new peer-to-peer payment technology.

Yet, none of the world's current digital payment systems like PayPal, Alipay, Apple Pay, Google Pay or Facebook's proposed Libra are the same as Bitcoin. They are centralized. The other seven thousand or so alternative coins are centralized entities too, with single points of failure. Bitcoin is a decentralized network with no single point of failure.

Satoshi designed Bitcoin's decentralized global blockchain in a manner that does not require a central or governing authority. This unique decentralized architectural design results in Bitcoin

being resistant to attempts by governments, tyrants

or any other entities to control, manipulate or turn

the Bitcoin network off[12]. Once Satoshi launched

the open-source software for Bitcoin, the genie

could not be put back in the bottle.

Satoshi described his Bitcoin network

invention as being robust in its simplicity and it

solved the world's final two problems for a viable

type of digital money. The double-spending

problem and the Byzantine General's problem.

For decades computer scientists and game

theorists around the world had been working on a

---

[12] Bitcoin: A Primer for Policymakers 2013 by Jerry Brito, Andrea
Castillo, and the Mercatus Center at George Mason University

digital cash that could prevent bad actors from double spending it. The second monumental task that they faced was designing something highly valuable that could operate from any point on the globe and could instantly move to any other place on the globe without being interfered with or altered in any manner.

Powered and Secured by Energy

Before going further into Bitcoin, it is important to add that Bitcoin is powered and secured by energy. Since math does not carry the ambiguity sometimes found in written languages, the brute mathematics behind Bitcoin can be as easily quantified, understood and proven as measuring electric input and output.

Just as the measurable electrical impulses of the human heart and brain gives credence to proof-of-life in humans, the measurable electronic processing power required to secure and process

Bitcoin transactions can be validated by the processing power required to sustain it.

Like an atomic heart, the amount of electrical energy power required to secure and process Bitcoin transactions is measured in real-time and virtually self-audited every 10 minutes, giving the world both credence and proof that Bitcoin is working.[13]

This means that the processing power of the computers driving the Bitcoin network is scientifically and precisely measured to pinpoint mathematically provable data that the network is

---

[13] Written Testimony- Hearing of the U.S. Senate Energy and Natural Resources Committee (August 21, 2018) by Thomas A. Golden Program Manager, Technology Innovation Electric Power Research Institute.

recording, validating and confirming transactions while also preventing bad actors from double spending or spending the same money twice. At any given moment, Bitcoin's trustworthiness can be proved in cases where honesty and transparency are important.

The Bitcoin network has more security and processing power than the world's five largest supercomputers, making it the most secure operating network on the globe[14]. Thousands of earth-based and a handful of space based decentralized Bitcoin nodes and millions of Bitcoin mining computers around the world broadcast, record, validate, confirm, audit and

---

[14] How Much Power It Takes to Create a Bitcoin by Danny Bradbury updated April 22,2020. Thebalance.com

publish all Bitcoin transactions 24 hours a day and

produces one block of transaction data and a

specific number of Bitcoin every 10 minutes. Each

Bitcoin is representative of 100,000,000 smaller

singular digital units. Its value rest in the

immutable grantee of its security and the amount

of electrical energy that was required to create it.[15]

A digital asset such as this makes Bitcoin a

highly valuable digital asset is cases where an

intermediary, arbitrator or authority is not required

in order to establish security, transparency and

validity. And, since this asset is digital it is able to

operate atop the Internet or via a communications

---

[15] https://cointelegraph.com/explained/proof-of-work-explained by Andrew Tar (January 2018)

device it is usable in the developed world and in developing countries.

The Bitcoin blockchain mines or creates 6.25 Bitcoin every 10 minutes and will produce half as many every four years until the year 2140.

Anyone who chooses can create or mine Bitcoin by leasing or buying Bitcoin mining computers and downloading the free open-source software on the Internet but energy cost considerations can be a big factor.

Today, it is far less expensive for private individuals to purchase a fraction of a Bitcoin than it is for them to try and mine a Bitcoin unless they are already mining Bitcoin in a large pool of miners.

A Bitcoin is not physical but digital in nature. Bitcoin's cryptographic addressing message containment cubicle is a string of about 34 cryptographic alpha numeric numbers and letters that look similar to this:

1ERx6TeSKKhpfhA3x7EXdmunJTHy1QkGa2.[16]

Once a Bitcoin is mined, created or rewarded it automatedly goes into the Bitcoin miner's wallet where it is stored until the miner decides to move it. The miner is able to pay someone with it, sell it to someone in exchange for fiat currency, purchase goods or services or trade it in-exchange for something else. There are also

---

[16] Actual bitcoin wallet public address.

computer applications being developed for Bitcoin and cryptocurrency lending.

Since there is no method for a Bitcoin miner to be rewarded for securing and processing Bitcoin transactions without converting the required amount of energy into processing power there is no incentive for them to game the network. Any who attempt to attack the Bitcoin network can be easily detected and/or ignored by the network. Thus, it is more profitable for them to play fair than it is for them to attack the network.[17]

Bitcoin is the world's first decentralized digital remunerations tool. While Bitcoin does not

[17] Rui Zhang, Rui Xue, and Ling Liu. 2019. Security and Privacy on Blockchain. ACM Computer. Survey. 1, 1, Article 1 (January 2019), 35 pages. https://doi.org/10.1145/3316481

exist in the physical ream it dominates our global land, sea and air scape because it is immune from distance as well as geographical barriers. It operates intertwined with the Internet as a consensus driven, global-decentralized cryptographic network with no single point of control and no single point of failure. Just like the Internet.

Bitcoin's level of security and processing power can be monitored and measured by observing the hash rate of the Bitcoin network. Recently it has been around 105 trillion tera hashes[18] per second. This means computers that are processing and validating Bitcoin transactions

---

[18] Blockchain.com - 1 tera hash is 1 trillion hashes per second.

are also making a combined 105 trillion guesses

per second in a race to determine which mining

pool wins the transactions block by finding a

nonce number.

It is akin to solving a puzzle because once

the puzzle is completed, everyone can determine

that it is correct. This guessing game requires

Bitcoin mining resources, computer processing

time and energy power and is called proof-of-

work.

This winning hashed nonce is said to have

been difficult because of the proof-of-work that

had to have been accomplished in order to be

awarded for the block. The winning hashed block

is difficult to produce but easy to verify and

validate. After a block is awarded, all mining computers quickly signal confirmation and work begins on the next block. This process repeats itself every 10 minutes, 24 hours a day, seven days a week.

Decentralized Platform of Trust

Bitcoin can best be thought of as a computerized platform of trust that is accessible by a person or a machine. It lives in an environment were all its transactions are publicly broadcasted. The platform is decentralized, therefore no one data center exercises command and control over the network.

Its network is made up of thousands of nodes and mining computers that record, broadcast and validate all its transactions. The platform possesses futuristic security features that detect and punishes bad actors and attackers who repeatedly submit invalid transactions. The platform is resilient and the more it is attacked, the stronger it becomes because it is antifragile. Each day of operation brings a step-up in security and sudden price dives help to drive away speculators and widens distribution to more network participants.

Secondly, the platform audits and broadcast a confirmed report every 10 minutes along with its irreversible historical record.

Imagine also that this platform of trust interacts with cryptographic tokens that humans can transfer or exchange between themselves simply by using an electronic device such as a mobile phone, tablet or computer. And, because

the native cryptographic tokens used on the

platform are scarce, impossible to counterfeit and

digitally programmable, they are considered useful

as a medium of exchange in cases where trust is

paramount. This empowers human decisions.

The more accustomed we become to this

new digital age, the more apparent it becomes that

we are indeed transitioning into an era of freedom

from serving the interest of corrupt financial

intermediaries and bankers. Just as horses, oxen

and horse drawn carriages faded as the automobile

emerged as the primary means of transportation,

fiat money is posed to fade as Bitcoin becomes

more widely distributed.

Computer scientists and programmers who contribute to the Bitcoin protocol claim that it is the most secure programable cryptographic network in the world.[19] Its growth has been organic and without management and control of a single person or entity.

Bitcoin is difficult to explain, and even more difficult to understand because it has other characteristics that help shape and define its nature. It is useful to view it as a platform of trust because it isn't money (as we know it) and the blockchain technology that undergirds it isn't a system of currency. It's not a company, it's not a

---

[19] A Survey on Security and Privacy Issues of Bitcoin. Dec. 25,2017.

product, it's not a service or something you need to sign-up for.

Going further, Bitcoin is the concept of a decentralized platform of trust that can be applied to the way humans communicate value - or to what we call – money[20]. It opens up a universe where human value transaction can originate from one point on earth and be instantly transferred to a human or a machine on any continent with no friction or permission needed from anyone. As an absolute example, anyone in the world is free to set-up and run a full Bitcoin network node without seeking anyone's approval or permission.[21]

---

[20] *The Internet of Money* (2016) by Andreas Antonopoulos
[21] Bitcoin.org

In order to arrive at this celestial level of trust, Satoshi's Bitcoin protocol solved the decades long Byzantine General's Problem – that of transferring valuable information across distances and through obstacles - and the modern-day banking problem of bad actors spending the same dollar twice. Computer scientists and game theorists around the world had been working on solving these problems but no one had achieved success until Satoshi proved it with Bitcoin.

Satoshi[22] proved that cryptographic transactions could be broadcasted over a decentralized global network where consensus agreement must be achieved in order for any

---

[22] https://bitcoin.org/bitcoin.pdf

transaction to be considered valid. It dictates that all non-validated transactions or transactions containing changes be ignored.

Satoshi also proved that the cryptographic transactions taking place on this platform of trust - would be so secure that bad actors would have to achieve the equivalent of traveling back in time in order to erase or change any past Bitcoin transactions.   Although they may try, it cost more for bad actors to attack the Bitcoin protocol than it does for them to play fair.

Bitcoin's cryptographic makeup makes it possible for users to trust that the underlying blockchain technology is able to transfer value - while ensuring the sender's and receiver's authenticity - and the validity of their currency. So, by using the Bitcoin standard protocol, we are merely trusting the proof of the math in our value transactions.

Assured trust in Bitcoin's blockchain technology begins with its digital cryptographic architecture. Even when a Bitcoin public digital signature or address is known it cannot be deciphered or put to any useful purpose by bad actors. This is because the public signature or public address is cryptographically paired to a private signature or private key known only by the person or machine who owns or controls it.

And, yes even a machine or a computer can own Bitcoins. There is no discrimination or bias in

Bitcoin. Bitcoin public signatures and addresses can only be used to receive Bitcoin inputs which makes it impossible for outsiders to hack or to cause it to send Bitcoins out. Only with the paired private signature keys or address can a Bitcoin be moved or spent.

Bitcoin the Super Commodity

As we have seen Bitcoin is an instrument of near endless proportions but nowhere does it shine more brightly than in the observational light of its characteristic as a commodity[23].

Commodities come in many forms such as beans, corn, rice, hogs and cows. There are other commodities like plastic bottles, straws and chemicals. More expensive commodities would include gold and iron ores. These all have things in

---

[23] US Commodity Futures Trading Commission. Commodity Exchange Act (CEA) cftc.gov

common such a fungibility or being just like any other in its category.

This similarity among like commodities gives rise to competition among and between those who supply it and those who demand or want to purchase it. These competing parties constitute a market's value and its value at any given time will naturally trend toward a state of efficiency and equilibrium between its supply and demand price points.

When operating in a free market, commodity price points drift toward a balancing point between its supply and what the market is willing to pay. When a commodity supply and demand price points are in balance in its overall market, it is said to be in a state of equilibrium.

Like the tugging of gravity and weightlessness, these two market forces are constantly at odds. If the rate of supply increases faster than the rate of demand then suppliers are likely to react by lowering price points to reward for decreasing demand.

Conversely, if the rate of demand increases faster than the rate of supply then suppliers are likely to react by increasing price points to reward for the increasing demand.

But Bitcoin is no ordinary commodity. Over the last 11 years, Bitcoin has proven itself to be a super commodity. Bitcoin is not yet a substitute for the legal tinder of any of the world's leading countries but it enjoys the same trading rights in the global commodities marketplace as pork bellies, beans, gold, crude oil and fiat money.

But unlike pork bellies, beans, gold, crude oil or any other commodities, Bitcoin is the world's rarest. With its hard-coded cryptographic algorithm, the world only has 21 million at its disposal.[24]

So far, some 18.5 million Bitcoins have been mined or created. Today, only 900 Bitcoins are supplied daily according to its hard-coded cryptographic algorithm. While we may not know

---

[24] https://decrypt.co/34876/why-is-bitcoins-supply-limit-set-to-21-million by Daniel Phillips (July 2020)

how many tons of pork bellies or beans will come to market each day, it is a sure bet that only 900 Bitcoin will be supplied each day and the number will halve every four years for the next 120 years. This finite level of scarcity separates Bitcoin from every other commodity on planet earth.

Benefiting from sure-winning bets on Bitcoin comes with a certain level of responsibility because not all market participants act morally or rationally and Bitcoin's game-theory is based on long-time time preference rather than quick gain. Bitcoin may be a super commodity but if you bet more on it than you can afford to lose you may not be acting morally or rationally and you will get (REKT) wrecked.

Very few Bitcoin users have become instantly wealthy and many looking for instant gratification have lost fortunes. Failing to know the difference between Bitcoin and other digital commodities in its class invites other hazards.

If the finite level of scarcity separates Bitcoin from other commodities on earth, the massive cost of creating it separates it even more. Take gold and oil for example. The annual extractable gold supply is about 3,200 metric tons or 7 million pounds.[25] Experts put gold production cost between $1,000- $1,200 per ounce, and oil production cost at about $1.50 per gallon.

---

[25] World Gold Council. Gold.org

Experts put Bitcoin production cost at around $4,000 per Bitcoin. Commodities that have low production cost or that can be easily produced usually have lower values on the economic spectrum.

Due to the fair game theory hard-coded into the Bitcoin protocol, the available supply and the market demand is flowing constantly through time and can suddenly become very expensive for sending small amounts of Bitcoin. Therefore, transaction cost rise as the market moves toward equilibrium when the network is handling higher than usual volume.

Fiat Money

Fiat money can best be described as the currency used by national governments and a nation's banking regulatory system. Together, these two-partner institutions develop plans and policies to manage its national and sometimes another nation's fiat monetary system. Management is usually done in a manner that is good enough to satisfy people's confidence in using it as a medium of exchange and a store of value.

And of course, a government's requirement to use it as a legal tender for paying taxes is its primary strength. When it comes to other nations, sometimes military might, coercion or dictatorial control are employed to inspire confidence in the US dollar (USD).

The other main reasons we use fiat money as a medium of exchange is because it is widely distributed, easily dividable, easy to store and easy to secure and transport. Due to its former link with gold, we also associate it with being desirable as a store of value. We also desire it because authorities do a good job of preventing and combating bad actors who attempt to counterfeit it.

Unlike the rest of the world, we in America have become comfortable with using fiat paper bills even as newer forms of fiat products like bank and corporate owned debit, credit and payment cards have been introduced. Still, new fiat money like Automated Clearing House Network (ACH) products, Direct Deposit, direct pay, bill pay and electronic check have grown in popularity.

Even more recently mobile phone banking applications are growing in popularity and various banking Apps are becoming popular in transacting the movement of fiat money. Some allow for using Bitcoin. This new phenomenon has developed as a result of advancements in communications technology, expanding growth of web connectivity and growing awareness of the power of Bitcoin.

Since Bitcoin's DNA is digital, it works naturally by using bar codes on mobile phones. As a digital asset tool, Bitcoin's blockchain technology holds promise that it may one day be common sense to eliminate not only fiat money but also banks and third-party financial interlopers in our value transactions.

Paper fiat money bills benefit from their legacy status but have been losing their underlying credibility, practicality and value as time passes.

Gold-backed US dollars reigned supreme until President Richard Nixon totally abandoned the gold benchmark amid the nation's war debts, politics at home, shifting geopolitics in the Middle East and world oil energy crisis in 1971.

Today, the US dollar (USD) has gotten to the point where it is really nothing more than accounting numbers which are transferred between financial institutions, governments, businesses and consumers. The physical supply of paper fiat money is relatively small compared to the massive amount of digital money that exist on computer statements.

Fiat money has also been undermined by fraud, lack of transparency in the financial industry and the necessity of central banks and governments to continuously print ever-increasingly massive amounts of it to maintain public confidence.[26]

Greed and repeating cycles of dollar devaluation have also helped to destroy the US dollar's usefulness as store of value as evidenced by miniscule to no interest on savings accounts. Not only are the wages of American workers near stagnate, but we are caught in the savings dilemma as well.

The practice of shrinkflation on the part of the grocery and food packaging industry has further obscured the fact that we are receiving less

---

[26] Boston Consulting Group: Banks paid $321 billion in fines since financial crisis. Reuters Report March 2, 2017.

grocery products for more cost when it comes to the US dollar (USD) at home.

Moreover, less than one percent of the US population owns and control more wealth or total US dollar supply than the bottom 90 percent of the population combined.[27] The consequences of this gross inequality alone should give us pause in trusting fiat money to solve our problems in the future. So, we must begin considering Bitcoin now because leading economists are ringing alarms and sounding warnings about the wealth gap, the massive supply of dollars being printed and the growing US debt.[28]

---

[27] Credit Suisse Global wealth report 2019. Credit-suisse.com
[28] *Capitalism Hits the Fan* (2013) by Richard Wolff.

Where does a dollar come from? Modern monetary theory suggest that fiat money creation begins through a complex process whereby money is deposited in a bank. The bank then holds a fraction of the deposit in reserve and lends the rest to borrowers. The borrowers deposit the funds and the process repeats itself over and over throughout the economy. A more complex appendage considers the role of central banks in monitoring and regulating these processes.

While this money creation -- by fractional reserve explains the apparent ongoing flow of new money, it is far from the truth. Fiat money creation is much simpler and straight forward. It begins with Federal Reserve bankers sitting around a conference table holding meetings and taking

votes.[29] As a result of these meetings, the

designated Federal Reserve designee hits keys on a

computer keyboard and money is instantly created.

In contrast, a more complex appendage considers

the role of the US Treasury in printing the

greenbacks and trading government bonds.

As we can see, the process is far simpler and

more arbitrary than one might think. Since fiat

money is technically debt, it can be used to

manipulate and subjugate vast populations as in

the case of African Americans and the population

of poorer, weaker nations.

---

[29] Board of Governors of the Federal Reserve System. Federal Open
Market Committee Minutes. federalreserve.gov

Sound Money

As we have seen, money is a tool. In this respect, Bitcoin is also a tool. Fiat money can be programed to work on top of Bitcoin as a medium of exchange and store of value.   In addition, the security, transparency, decentralized ledger and the cryptographic technology that underpins Bitcoin makes it a superior unit of account and useful as a sound money.

Whereas, the supply and demand for fiat money is controlled and regulated by a handful of people, the supply of Bitcoin is fixed and the demand is created by the masses of people who value and use it.

Bitcoin is a sound money because it can be used as a store of value and as a medium of exchange. Moreover, it does not require a bank or intermediaries for transaction approval which makes its fungibility as a unit of account absolute. Whether individuals prefer to use Bitcoin or not, it has no effect on its supply. If one does not own it or use it, one cannot benefit from it.

One of the first qualities for a sound money is a scarce supply. It must also be difficult and expensive to produce. If the supply of a certain medium of exchange is abundant, then its abundancy would drive down its value much like the abundancy of seashells, salt and beads led to their demise as a money tool.

In addition, a sound money must also be able to perform as a store of value. Its value must be likely to increase over periods of time. Gold is considered a sound money because of its limited supply and resulting rises in value over time.

Due to exploration and mining expenses, only 2,500 tons of gold is mined each year.[30] The production cost, together with scarcity has made gold, the world's premier sound money.

---

[30] World Gold Council Report (2020). Gold.org

Gold's use in jewelry, communication devices, luxury furnishings and other industrial uses as well as its ability to be recycled contributes to its status as sound money - and valuable commodity.

As we have learned, prior to the 1970s, the US dollar (USD) was linked to gold. After eliminating the linkage, the same law granted central bankers and government regulators the right to print unrestricted amounts of fiat money at will. Not only has this hyper-printing of the US dollar gotten out of hand but social and technological progress since the 1970s are rapidly outstripping central bankers and government officials' ability to control it or keep track of it.

The overprinting and constant devaluating of fiat money has also resulted in failed policy solutions and a death spiral.

Despite losing its store of value proposition, hopefully fiat money is years away from collapsing as a medium of exchange. A slow methodical death for fiat money should give Bitcoin more time for infrastructure building and mass adoption.

Bitcoin exhibits the same positive characteristics we expect from gold except Bitcoin is not physical in nature, but digital. Whereas standardized gold pieces can be physically altered by chipping away the edges, Bitcoin is sent and received through cryptographic data communications technology and cannot be erased or altered, once transferred.

Finally, Bitcoin holds store of value and medium of exchange characteristics that gives it versatility as sound money.

In this digitized and globalized age where it is becoming customary to conduct transactions digitally, many innovators see the advances in technology as a natural opportunity to adapt Bitcoin as the sound money for the future.

Bitcoin Solutions

As we have learned, in its first year of existence Bitcoin was rather obscure. A year later a buyer purchased two pizzas for 10,000 BTC in a noteworthy transaction that briefly captured worldwide media attention. It didn't take long for cyberpunks, cryptographers, computer programmers, computer scientists and game theorists to begin examining its design and architecture.

Satoshi's whitepaper, which was written in English was soon translated into other languages. With its free and open Internet protocol word soon spread around the world about its remarkable characteristics.

As the apparent value of Bitcoin as a commodity and medium of exchange -- that acted like money-- spread globally, Bitcoin users, traders and educators picked up the Bitcoin banner.

As the years, months, weeks, days, hours, minutes and seconds of Bitcoin's uninterrupted operation tick away as designed, there is a global race to develop it as a technology solution to many of the world's problems.

And, since one has to purchase or earn

Bitcoin to experiment with it as a sound money

proposition, the supply and demand for it has been

rocky. And, it has risen from zero to $10,000 per

Bitcoin in 11 years.

Looking back, Bitcoin ended its first year

valued just over $0.10 per Bitcoin. It reached $17

per Bitcoin in 2011 before falling to $0.01.[31]

By 2013, it had roller-coasted to $31.91

before moving up to $100 per Bitcoin. By 2017, it

had reached $20,000 per Bitcoin. Its trade value

has ebbed and flowed on global exchanges just like

the trade value for pork bellies, beans, gold and

---

[31]   https://www.investopedia.com/articles/forex/121815/bitcoins-price-history.asp

crude oil. It has out-performed them by vast margins.

Today Bitcoins trade hands at about $10,000 USD per Bitcoin[32] and its market capitalization is about $180 billion in US dollars or roughly the same size value as Intel Corp, one the largest multinational semiconductor chip manufactures in the world.

Confidence in Bitcoin's blockchain technology has grown and its level of success has attracted new waves of attention each year. The level of success being attained today by new industries building business models around Bitcoin

---

[32] https://www.tradingview.com/

is attracting yet another new wave of Bitcoiners from all walks of life who are educating and involving themselves in the Bitcoin community and using it to help themselves and in some cases, using it to solve world problems.

There is no reason why African Americans should not be exploring Bitcoin solutions to address our economic concerns. From accumulating Sats, to participating in building Bitcoin and crypto structured business models, there is plenty space for exploration with high chances of success.

True to its character, Bitcoin remains indifferent to being the center of attention. With no central controller or authority in charge, there is no place to go to ask for permission to get involved. And, since the Internet has to be shut down in order to turn Bitcoin off, it might be around for quite some time.

Bitcoin has a proven record of success in peer-to-peer transactions like family and friend remittances and international value transfers. Some users and new companies look to Bitcoin for inflation hedges, IRAs[33], store of value asset, trading opportunities and HODLING which is buying and "holding on to Bitcoin for dear life."

Make no mistake, Bitcoin is still in its infancy and its infrastructure is years away from

---

[33]https://www.bitira.com/fidelity-and-bitcoin-a-process-of-cryptocurrency-adoption-since-2014/

maturity. It will have to go through the same growth stages for widespread global adaption just as electricity, telephone, television, computer and other great world inventions.

One only need to look back to the history of those world transforming inventions to reason that Bitcoin offers a new frontier for progressive African Americans because of Black America's contributions to the success of those technologies over the last 100 years was instrumental in their success.

Crypto Terminology

In gaining knowledge to any subject matter it is always useful to have a basic understanding of the vocabulary and terminology used by early adapters to help quicken your learning experience. Some key words and redefined terms are listed in this chapter.

2FA or 2 Factor Authentication: An additional layer of security that requires information only the owner can produce to show proof.

Fifty-one Percent Attack (51% Attack): A concerted evil-intentioned effort by an organized person or group to overtake and control more than half the blockchain computing power with an ability to manipulate transactions to benefit themselves.

Algorithm: A series of steps needed to solve a problem.

Alternative Coin: Any cryptocurrency other than Bitcoin.

Anonymous: Unknown person or group.

Anti-money Laundering or AML: A set of laws aimed at monitoring and preventing the ability of citizens and foreigners to convert

illegally gained money into money that appears to

have been earned legally.

ASIC or Application Specific Integrated Circuit Miner: A computer chip designed specifically to record Bitcoin transactions onto the Bitcoin blockchain.

Atomic Swap: Technology that allows exchanging different cryptocurrencies between individuals.

Bear Market: A market environment in which commodity prices are generally trending downward.

Bit: The smallest unit of a digital product that can be deduced in the form 0 or 1.

Bitcoin: A cryptographic digital product unit that is capable of recording and maintaining a decentralized ledger of its outputs and inputs.

Bitcoin ATM: An automated vending machine that exchanges Bitcoin and fiat money.

Block: A digital record created within the blockchain that is linked to the past, present and future.

Blockchain: Pages of permanent and highly secure records of Bitcoin transactions that have been confirmed and proved to be irreversible on the Bitcoin network by consensus agreement.

Block Reward: A certain amount of Bitcoin awarded to Bitcoin miners for processing, securing and broadcasting Bitcoin transactions approximately every ten minutes.

Blockchain Explorers: Websites that broadcast Bitcoin data and provide tools for exploring various spaces in the Bitcoin ecosystem.

BOT: A computer program that automates an action.

Bull Market: A market environment in which commodity prices are generally trending upward.

Byzantine Generals' Problem: A warlike environment where security, time and distance are constant challenges to organization and coordination between units and where no valuable messages can be trusted.

Cash: A physical paper money or digital representation issued by a bank or corporation.

Centralized: An organized company or system of governance that is controlled by one person or a group of people.

Circulating Supply: The number of coins currently available and in the hands of people.

Code: Information that is apparently unreadable but can be made readable.

Cold Storage: Digital data that is not connected to the Internet.

Confirmation: An evident proof that a transaction was recorded and verified on the Bitcoin blockchain.

Consensus: General agreement amongst a majority of at least 51% of a group or community.

Crypto: A short word for cryptography.

Cryptocurrency: An electronic or digital money that uses technology and digital algorithms to control its supply.

Cryptography: Branch of mathematics that secures information by hiding and rendering it unreadable without a code, key and proven mathematical identity to unlock.

DApp: A decentralized application as in a public software application that runs on a network of computers with no point or points of central control.

Darkweb: That part of the World Wide Web that is not indexed by web search engines.

Decentralized: A system consisting of independent parts of a network with no central authority or central controller.

Digital: Electronic technology that uses the digits 0 and 1 in its operation.

Digital Asset: Any digitally generated product such as a document, file, photo, recording, crypto-key or such that any owner has a right to own or use.

Digital Signature: A permission or proof accomplished through a computer that signifies agreement by an authorized person.

Distributed Ledger: A network of independent computers that are working in sync to record and validate transactions in a network.

Double Spend: A practice that deceitfully uses the same money to pay two parties but only pays one or neither if the scheme is completed.

Dust Transaction: Very small amounts of satoshis or fractions of Bitcoin of other cryptocurrencies.

Encryption: Locking information in coded form such that it is unreadable without a key or code.

Ethereum: The second largest and most popular open-source cryptocurrency besides Bitcoin that was proposed and created by Vitalik Buterin in 2015.

Fiat Currency: Money that has been declared by a government or central bank to have value.

FOMO: Short form for fear of missing out.

Fork: An occurrence when two or more blocks are discovered at the same time and begin propagating over the globe. The issue is resolved by the network recognizing the block with the longest chain.

FUD: Short form expression for fear, uncertainty and doubt.

Full Node: A computer in the Bitcoin network that has a complete and current copy of the blockchain ledger and is capable of validating transactions and new blocks.

Fungible: Possessing the quality wherein two or more of the same things have similar value and can be substituted interchangeably.

Genesis Block: The first block in a blockchain.

Hack: Usually the act of using one's computer to manipulate another computer or computer network to achieve a mischievous goal.

Halving: The occurrence every four years wherein there is a 50 percent reduction in miner rewards or new supply of Bitcoin creation.

Hardware Wallet: A device that secures Bitcoin or another cryptocurrency and can be disconnected from the internet.

Hash Function: A computing process that turns information into a series of numbers and letters of defined certain lengths.

Hash Rate: The measurable unit at which a computer of network of computers can take information and turn it into a series of numbers and letters of defined certain lengths.

HODL: A famously popular misspelling for "hold" that emerged in the crypto community as a meme to buy and hold on to Bitcoin for dear life no matter the fiat exchange rate.

ICO: Initial coin offering was a method used by individuals and firms to introduce alternative coins to Bitcoin into the marketplace.

Input: Bitcoin being received into a wallet.

Key: A string of alphanumeric characters or numbered words.

KYC or Know Your Customer: Customer identification requirements mandated by banking and financial laws, presumably to prevent money laundering.

Ledger: A book or record of account of all past and present transactions.

Lighting Network: A second layer digital network solution that operates atop the Bitcoin network.

Merkle Tree: A precise hashed mathematical visualization of organized data that would look similar to the root, trunk, branches, stems and leaves of a tree.

Microtransaction: An online transaction involving very small amount of money or value.

Mining: The process of using computers to help securely record, validate and confirm Bitcoin transactions in the hopes of next being rewarded for being the first computer in the network to solve a complex mathematical problem within the block of transactions.

Mining Difficulty: A measure of the computer processing power required to increase the chances of solving a complex mathematical problem within a block of transactions at any given time.

Mining Pool: A group of people or firms who combine their computer processing power to increase their overall chance of solving a complex mathematical problem within a block of transactions and share the rewards.

Mining Rig: One or more mining computers.

Money: Any tool in a system of units that can be used for exchanging value.

Moore's Law: A theory that calculates computer technology development and advancement.

Mt. Gox: The first widely used online website where Bitcoin could be exchanged for fiat money.

Multisignature: A system wherein two or more digital approvals are required before a transaction can be recorded.

Node: Any computer powered device that is broadcasting and receiving data in the Bitcoin network.

Nonce: A precise and correctly determined random number that was arrived at by guess work and can be easily proven to be true and correct by simple math calculations or observation.

Open Source: Computer technology that has been made publicly available for sharing by anyone and can be used and modified at will and cannot be subjected to any permissions for its use.

Output: Bitcoin going out of a wallet.

P2P: Short form for peer-to-peer, whereas the peers in the network are equal persons, devices or entities with neither enjoying advantages, rights or privileges in the network.

Paper Wallet: A single piece or sheet of paper used to store seed phrases or private keys that can be used to electronically access Bitcoin when keyed into a computer communications device.

Payee: The person who receives money once it is transmitted.

Peer-to-Peer: From one equal person, device or entity to another within a network wherein no person, device or entity enjoys any advantages, rights or privileges in the network.

Permissionless: A state or situation in which anyone can participate without having to

seek any anyone's permission, approval or
authorization.

Platform: An electronic environment
operated and governed by computer software
protocols.

Ponzi Scheme: A fake business enterprise
that draws in investors and business opportunity
seekers but has little to no significant designs to
produce business profits but rather uses new
investors and participants to compensate older
ones.

POS: Short for Proof of Stake or the process
of achieving blockchain network consensus
wherein participants cannot spend or move certain

amounts of their token holdings for the chances to be rewarded fees for using their computing power to process and validate transactions.

POW: Short for Proof of Work or the process of achieving blockchain network consensus wherein participants compete with each other in solving puzzle-like computations for chances to be rewarded fees for using their computing power to process and validate transactions.

Private Key: String of Bitcoin alphanumeric characters or seed words known only by the owner.

Public Address: String of Bitcoin alphanumeric characters and also QRC code that identifies a Bitcoin wallet.

Public Key: String of Bitcoin alphanumeric characters and also QRC code that allows Bitcoin to be received.

Pump and Dump: A manipulation strategy wherein an individual, group or firm conspires to drive up the price of a commodity so that they can then rapidly sell at high prices.

Pyramid Scheme: A scam that makes money by drawing in investors and business opportunity seekers and relies on them to recruit new participants to successfully operate but has little to no significant designs to produce business profits but rather uses new investors and participants to compensate older ones.

QR: Short for quick response code, a square shaped barcode that is used for scanning and relaying electronic data.

Regulated: Commercial activity that is controlled and supervised by government rules and sometimes directly monitored by government employees and agents.

Regulation: Rules, directives and laws that uses force such as fines and penalties as the means to control activity.

REKT: The intentional missed spelling for wrecked, meaning financially crushed or ruined.

Remittance: A sum of money sent, especially to support family, also as payment for goods and services. Such transfers usually require financial intermediaries.

Satoshi: Smallest unit of a Bitcoin, one-hundred millionth of a Bitcoin, 0.00000001 in honor of Satoshi Nakamoto.

Satoshi Nakamoto: The writer of the open-sourced Bitcoin technology protocol.

Scamcoin: A fake coin, usually posing as a cryptocurrency for the purpose of misleading, confusing and stealing from the unsuspecting

public.

SEC: Short for Securities and Exchange

Commission is an independent US government

agency that is responsible for protecting investors

and maintaining fair and ordered functioning of the

securities and capital markets.

SHA-256: One of the most technologically

secure ways to protect digital information by

processing it into irreversible 256-Bit

alphanumeric characters.

Shitcoin: A derogatory term for a

centralized alternative coin, especially if it lacks

any advanced distributive technology.

Side Chain: Emerging technology being developed to run parallel to the Bitcoin network as connected side rail networks handling speedy micro transactions that do not necessarily require the security, number of transaction confirmations and time in return for lower transaction fees.

Silk Road: One of the world's largest and most successful commercial enterprises that accepted Bitcoin between 2011-2013 and was later found to be an illegal operation.

Smart Contract: An agreement to transact an exchange of commodities, goods or services that will execute automatically and so long as certain conditions are met and functions without a third-party oversight or mediation.

Soft Fork: A consensus mechanism for the Bitcoin network wherein any software upgrade change remains compatible with the older version.

TestNet: An experimental Bitcoin network environment used by anyone, including engineers and computer scientists to experiment with new ideas without endangering the Bitcoin network.

Token: A digital asset representative of itself or something real-world.

Total Supply: The amount of available cryptocurrency coins.

Transaction: The transfer of fiat money or cryptocurrency from one person to another.

Transaction Fee: Payment to the person or business providing the security and infrastructure for transactions.

Transaction ID: A distinct string of alphanumeric characters used to identify an exchange of money or Bitcoin between two parties.

Trustless: Such a high-quality standard that parties need not require trust among themselves or an arbitrator to conduct a transaction.

Unbanked: Individuals, communities or businesses who do not have access to banking services.

Utility Token: A digital unit that allows electronic access to a game, a product or a service.

Verification: The process that confirms a transaction has been recorded on the Bitcoin blockchain.

Wallet: A software product that communicates with the Bitcoin blockchain and allows users and merchants to send and receive Bitcoin.

Whitepaper: A document designed to explain a product or service in such a manner that its premises can be independently checked and rigorously analyzed or evaluated.

Proof-of-Work

When Satoshi designed Bitcoin, she employed proof-of work and decentralization concepts in its architecture. These two technologies were not new scientific concepts but essential ingredients for making Bitcoin a provably-fair gambit with a formidably defended public ledger with no single point failure.

Various characteristics of "proof-of-work" in Bitcoin can be found. For example, there is proof of work in its existence. The ability to open a Bitcoin wallet and see the amount of Bitcoin can be considered as proof that it exists. Every newly created Bitcoin comes with a traceable permanent public record of the work that was required in its creation. This cryptographic math record, by its very nature validates the Bitcoin as real.

However, the real power of Bitcoin is that a Bitcoin mining computer has to instantly produce proof that their mining computers performed a certain amount of energy power in processing computational work in order to be awarded Bitcoin. This proof-of-work information is publicly available on the Bitcoin blockchain and becomes a link for building the next block of transactions on the blockchain.

Scaling Bitcoin

According to Bitcoin critics, its inability to scale is a weakness. Whether it is discussing the size of a Bitcoin block or the number and speed of Bitcoin transactions on the Bitcoin blockchain, they say that these pillars of Bitcoin's architecture make it weak.

Meanwhile, Bitcoin optimists say that Bitcoin block sizes are adequate as demonstrated by Bitcoin Cash (BCH), a forked version of Bitcoin (BTC). Bitcoin Cash was created by

Bitcoiners who failed to get a community consensus back in 2015 for larger block sizes. Since then, there has been little to no meaningful advantages for Bitcoin Cash as evidenced by market values. Thus, the Bitcoin block size debate has been settled at Satoshis Nakamoto's original 1-4 MB range. It was a huge win for Satoshi's philosophic consensus mechanisms during those early day Bitcoin debates and skirmishes.

Meanwhile, the Bitcoin Cash block size is 8MB and said to offer quicker validation and confirmation times but is considered centralized and less secure than Bitcoin. It joins thousands of other alternative coins that compete with Bitcoin in the cryptocurrency market space.

Meanwhile, the added security of limited size blocks and a slow pace for Bitcoin transactions has only added to its strength, resilience and performance.   Also, the scarcity of Bitcoin, together with its economically reliable transaction confirmation times ensures that participants in the Bitcoin blockchain network play fair and that Bitcoin transaction fees, if any, are transparent.

Looking back, in the first year or two after Bitcoin's creation the network transaction volume was low enough for users to be able to send and receive transactions that were less than a $0.01 in value or at no cost. But as network transaction volume increased users paid network transaction fees for faster transaction confirmation times.

While Bitcoin transaction fees are standard, Bitcoin sidechain network coders are developing technologies that operate seamlessly atop the Bitcoin network with little to no transaction fees for transfers between peers in the network.

These and other potential off chain solutions gives the community confidence that Bitcoin's scaling problem means opportunity for enterprises that can build popular applications atop the Bitcoin platform or atop its Lighting network[34].

---

[34] https://lightning.network/lightning-network-paper.pdf

Alternative Coins

Alternative coins or Alt coins are any cryptocurrencies other than Bitcoin. Alt coins do not run or operate on the Bitcoin blockchain.

Due to Bitcoin's early popular appeal among cryptographers, cyberpunks, computer scientists and the like, it did not take long for ideas to develop that sought to improve upon Bitcoin's open-source technology.

Research and development for these new alternatives emerged in various regions of the world with counties like Japan, South Korea, China, Germany, Czech Republic, and Austria leading the way in technical software development, user interfaces and economic study. The more resilient Bitcoin proved to be and the more successful it became added to the zeal of competing forces around the world.

Interestingly enough, many of the earliest alternative coins to Bitcoin were variations of Bitcoin. These variations were called forked coins. A few Bitcoin forked coins still exist. The most popular is Bitcoin Cash (BCH) which remains popular in Japan and respected around the world.

Alternative coins should not be taken lightly because the race for world dominance in the cryptocurrency technology space is just beginning. And, although Bitcoin reigns supreme in terms of decentralization, permissionless network, superior security and the like, competitors in the cryptocurrency industry are striving to top it. It also has the advantage of being the oldest and most successful cryptocurrency.

While no single alternative coin has yet come close to challenging the 105 trillion tera hashes per second processing power of the Bitcoin network, challengers still look for advantages in quicker transaction confirmation times, cheaper transaction fees, user anonymity and privacy features.

As we move into 2022, some of the world's largest Bitcoin inspired multi-national corporations, led by Facebook have announced plans to launch their own alternative coin. National governments in China, Dubai, Venezuela, Estonia, Sweden, and Japan have either already or will soon launch their own government backed alt coins, too. These competitors look to take advantage of already having a captive market of hundreds of millions of people and in some cases billions of prospective users.

Other alternative coin communities, both inside and outside government are attempting to design, launch and promote cryptocurrencies with the advantages of being backed by real property, luxury items, expensive artwork, diamonds and commodities like gold and oil.

Digital Gold and Sats Thinking

Most people have never heard of Bitcoin.

Many who have heard of it and have tried to buy it

probably found the experience to be a challenging

and self-learning adventure. As we have learned,

usage and handling are getting more user friendly

as new computer applications enter the

marketplace.

One reason educational initiatives and big

national marketing campaigns about Bitcoin are

not widespread is because no person or entity is in

charge of advertising and promoting it. The Bitcoin community is global and sparsely populated. The *Bitcoin Market Journal*, a trusted online newsletter estimates that of 8 billion people on the planet, less than 40 million people own any Bitcoin. Only 16 million Americans are said to own Bitcoin.

This relative unfamiliarity with Bitcoin presents opportunity for those who learn about it on their own and are early adaptors. No one does not have to ask anyone for permission to get involved with bitcoin, nor should anyone arrive late to the Bitcoin game.

As we have learned, Bitcoin is like digital gold. The best way to begin thinking about this new digital gold is thinking about it in satoshis, or sats for short.

Bitcoin has been likened to gold because gold has historically been recognized as the soundest form of money in the world. Both are rare and are limited in supply. They are hard to produce or mine and require security measurements to prevent theft.

While large quantities of gold are heavy and burdensome to transport or carry in our pockets, Bitcoin is physically weightless and travels digitally. And, while it is not practical to make smaller-unit exact change in gold transactions, breaking Bitcoin down into smaller units is not difficult.

As we have learned, a single Bitcoin (BTC) can be divided into 100,000,000 smaller units. You can also think of a Sat as one-one hundred millionth of a Bitcoin (BTC), 0.00000001 or 1/100,000,000.

Likewise, a single US dollar unit can be divided into 100 smaller units called cents, or pennies. A cent is one hundredth of a dollar, 0.01 or 1/100. In this technological age we must think sat-wise in order to be pennywise. To be pennywise means to be careful about the way we spend even small amounts of money. Besides its obvious weaknesses, the two-digit dollar is almost meaningless in a highly inflated and debt-ridden economy.

Bitcoin allows us to make our own moral decisions about how we choose to spend and save our chosen units of value. By thinking in sats we curb economic exploitation and fight a winnable struggle for Black Powernomics[35].

We can begin by transforming our minds to think in tens of millions rather than hundreds when thinking large. When we think units of value in the two-digit realm, we limit our ability to correctly analyze our present financial situation and adjust to a globalized economy relative to Bitcoin.

---

[35] Powernomics: The National Plan to Empower Black America (2001) by Dr. Claud Anderson

As the US dollar (USD) continues its downward slide as the world's reserve currency, we must also make sure we keep abreast of Bitcoin and crypto-technology as security against inflation.

Here's a counting chart to get a perspective on thinking tens of millions rather than hundreds based on one [is equal to] 10,000.

Sats Chart

1 BTC = 100,000,000 Satoshis

USD	Fraction	Number	Satoshi
$10,000*	1	1.00	100 million sats
$1,000*	1/10	0.10000000	10 million sats
$100*	1/100	0.01000000	1 million sats
$10*	1/1000	0.00100000	100,000 sats
$1*	1/10,000	0.00010000	10,000 sats
$0.10*	1/100,000	0.00001000	1,000 sats
$0.01	1/1,000,000	0.00000100	100 sats
$0.001	1/10,000,000	0.00000010	10 sats
$0.0001	1/100,000,000	0.00000001	1 sat

***If 1 BTC =$10,000**

The world supply of Bitcoin is capped at 21,000,000 and there are only about 900 Bitcoin mined each day and the amount will halve every four years, as we have learned.

As you can guess, there will never be enough Bitcoin for every American to own just one. This limited supply of Bitcoin points to the importance of beginning the process of educating ourselves about it, acquiring and working with Bitcoin (BTC) and sats in our everyday lives.

ACKNOWLEDGMENTS

I would like to thank Al and Ranjit Powell who introduced me to Bitcoin. Gavin Andresen, Andreas M. Antonopoulos, Sinclair Skinner, Saifedean Ammous, Arthur Hayes, Trace Mayer, Caitlin Long, Max Keiser, Roger "Bitcoin Jesus" Ver, Thomas Hunt of Mad Bitcoins, Tone Vays and Bitcoin developer Jimmy Song were among the many sources I looked to in my educating myself about Bitcoin. Dr. Claud Anderson inspired me reach out to Black people in laying out why this book should be written.

Ivan on Tech, I Love Black People, The Gentlemen of Crypto, Box Mining, UK Bitcoin Master, Cointelegraph, Data Dash, Davincij15, World Crypto Network, Peter McCormach, Sunny Decree and Off Chain with Jimmy Song are among the worldwide YouTube channels I have turned to in the last three years in studying Bitcoin.

I would like to thank my editor and my book cover image designer who both added to the quality of making this book better than what it otherwise might have been.

First and foremost, I thank my Lord, Jesus Christ.

Mail Order:
Phalconstar
PO Box 24
Greenville, TX 75403

Abcofbitcoin.org
$16.95 USD
0.00015 BTC
1ERx6TeSKKhpfhA3x7EXdmunJTHy1QkGa2

www.ingramcontent.com/pod-product-compliance
Lightning Source LLC
Chambersburg PA
CBHW050946050726
47592CB00007B/2459